THE
PERSONAL
CREDO
JOURNAL

THE

PERSONAL
CREDO
JOURNAL

A COMPANION TO

LEADING WITH **CHARACTER**
10 MINUTES A DAY TO A BRILLIANT LEGACY

DR. JIM LOEHR
WITH CAREN KENNEY

WILEY

For general information on our other products and services or for technical support, please contact our Customer Care Department within the United States at (800) 762-2974, outside the United States at (317) 572-3993 or fax (317) 572-4002.

Wiley publishes in a variety of print and electronic formats and by print-on-demand. Some material included with standard print versions of this book may not be included in e-books or in print-on-demand. If this book refers to media such as a CD or DVD that is not included in the version you purchased, you may download this material at http://booksupport.wiley.com. For more information about Wiley products, visit www.wiley.com.

Library of Congress Cataloging-in-Publication Data:

ISBN 9781119764069 (Paperback)
ISBN 9781119764083 (ePDF)
ISBN 9781119764076 (ePub)

COVER ART AND DESIGN: PAUL MCCARTHY

Printed in the United States of America
SKY10020878_090120

Contents

Introduction   1

    Final Notes   3

    Building Your Personal Credo   5

    Embedding Your Personal Credo and Supporting
It with Habits   97

    Additional Page for Journal Writing   158

Appendix A: Character Traits   177

Appendix B: Ranking Your Character Traits   181

Appendix C: Giver versus Taker Scale   183

Introduction

Welcome to your Personal Credo Journal and the beginning of an exercise and process that – if performed with the right focus and attention – may be one of the most important steps you take in creating your ultimate life and leadership legacy. A credo is a statement of beliefs and values that guides thinking, decisions, and behaviors. Many companies have instituted a credo or mission statement that is meant to define who they are as a company and guide the decisions and actions of their leadership and employees. While many leaders and individuals align with their company credo – and even adopt it as their own – very few have taken the time to focus on and create a Personal Credo.

The process of developing your Personal Credo begins with taking you deep within yourself, providing the opportunity to reflect on who you are, what you value and believe to be true, and what impact you want to have on the world around you. It highlights areas of vulnerability – where you are at risk of failing to thrive in your roles, relationships, and other areas of your life – and the potential disconnect between who you think you are, who you aspire to be, and how you want others to experience and remember you. In creating your Personal Credo document, you are adding the necessary level of thoughtfulness, deliberation, and intentionality to strengthening your character so that it enables you to become your best self and achieve your desired legacy.

Creating your Personal Credo takes time and requires thoughtful and intentional journaling for 10 minutes each day for a period of 90 days. You must actively resist the powerful urge to go through this process quickly, or you will not gain its profound benefit.

Before you undertake the construction of what will likely be the single most important navigational document in your life, the document against which your most important decisions and judgments will be vetted, please consider the following:

1. Personal Credo-building is deliberative and intentional. This thoughtful process requires you to set aside time in a quiet location to build and refine this document. If you speed through the steps, little, if anything, will come of it. As noted in the accompanying book *Leading with Character*, three to six weeks of dedicated training are required to increase the strength of physical muscles of the body. Strengthening character muscles and building the neurological architecture (neuropathways) supportive of those muscles take time, as well. Constructing a Personal Credo built to last and strong enough to withstand the forces of life simply cannot be done quickly. It will become a lifelong process of refining, re-calibrating, and re-evaluating. Failure to allow sufficient time for intentional, soulful, reflective pauses guarantees failure to lead with character.

2. The document you are about to create is the lens through which every important decision must be vetted. Because your Personal Credo represents the clearest, most accurate, self-determined articulation of your core beliefs, core values, mission, and purpose in life, it becomes your ultimate source code for determining right from wrong, and for navigating the storms of life.

3. Your Personal Credo is your best effort to rise above any flawed familial, cultural, or religious inputs; to transcend blind spots, sloppy thinking, faulty values and beliefs; to rigorously confront character weaknesses and imbalances; and to assume full responsibility for all decisions that impact your treatment of others.

4. Your Personal Credo is not a written document to be used as a reference guide. It is designed to be embedded at the core of your neuroprocessing system. It will become the centerpiece

of your worldview, your ultimate reality, your core mindset. It will become your internalized roadmap for a truly successful life.

5. Your Personal Credo represents the scorecard of highest value to you. When you score well, as measured by the dictates of this document, it means your life is fundamentally aligned with who you most aspire to be.

6. Included at the end of this journal is an additional 60-day exercise designed to help you bring your Personal Credo to life by loading it into your "moral operating system" and building habits to support it.

The mission targeted in your Personal Credo will take a lifetime to complete. Yet, excitingly, every single day represents one more opportunity to improve the skills needed to create your best self, your best life, your best legacy.

Final Notes

Caution: For some people, the first seven days of this training are particularly tough. Your Private Voice may try to convince you to abort the mission, describing it as a waste of time or too "touchy-feely." Disregard this negative messaging and continue forward. Anticipate and accept any discomfort when it comes, and just expect that, as with the building of physical muscle, you're unlikely to notice tangible results for the first couple of weeks or even more. Eventually, a shift takes place, and rather than your feeling as if you're forcing yourself to do the exercises, you will actually be drawn to them and miss it when you fail to work them into your daily routine.

• The creation of your Personal Credo is to be completed in as close to 90 days as possible. It is fine for you to write longer than 10 minutes – and some exercises are meant to be completed over multiple days – but 10 minutes is the minimum required for each day. Avoid completing multiple assignments at one time, or on the same day. Business travel, vacation days, personal emergencies should not exempt you from your training. If you miss a day or two, make up the assignments as soon as you can and do your best to stay on schedule.

- For those working with an executive coach: If you are unsure about a question or struggling with the exercise in some other way, make a note to discuss it with your coach. We also recommend checking in with your coach regularly to discuss key learning and insights.

- If the contents of your journal would be too damaging if read by certain others, tear out and shred those pages. We have found that this is the best solution to ensuring that clients get at the unvarnished truth in their self-exploratory writings. Extra pages, for additional writing, are included in the journal following the 90-day schedule, plus the 60-day follow-up. If necessary, use these pages to respond to the questions posed throughout this book, as well as to complete writing exercises suggested in the Character Call-Outs at the end of each chapter.

- Finally: You may wonder why examples of Personal Credos from our clients have not been provided here or in the accompanying *Leading with Character* book. Experience has shown us that examples have too much influence over our thinking. Rather than creating something completely original and authentic, we pick and choose what we like from the work of others. A Personal Credo must be uniquely crafted in a way that you alone could author. It can be 1 paragraph or 10, specific or general. This sacred document must be totally your creation.

Remember: a minimum of 10 minutes per day.

That's it!

Good luck, on arguably the most important journey of your life.

Building Your Personal Credo

(Days 1–90)

Day 1

What are the major themes in your life story thus far – such as overcoming obstacles, driven to succeed, fear of failure, negative private voice, never give up, low self-esteem, and so on?[1]

---

[1] Between 2006 and 2013, psychologist Fred Kiel conducted research on 84 CEOs from diverse industries. He found that leaders with high character, referred to as Virtuoso Leaders, were better able to recognize and weave together the threads of their life story to form a cohesive self-narrative. That's the intent of this writing. See Kiel, F. (2015). *Return on Character: The Real Reason Leaders and Their Companies Win*. Harvard Business Research Press, 54–55.

Day 2

What chapter headings best organize your life story thus far – such as "Overcoming Early Failure," "Building Confidence Through Sports," "Marrying Early," "How Parenthood Changed My View of the World," "My Academic Struggles," and so on?

Day 3

What are the six words that best describe the reality of your life thus far (e.g., determination, gratitude, driven, sacrifice, struggle, family)? Explain.

Days 4–5

What is the trajectory of your life story in the following areas? Is it getting better or worse?

1. Health (physical, emotional, mental, spiritual)
2. Happiness
3. Family
4. Leadership at work
5. Personal fulfillment
6. Moral character

Days 4–5 continued

Days 6–7

Write a synopsis of your life story up to the present day. Capture the most important themes and weave them together in a meaningful way.

Days 6–7 continued

Day 8

List eight words that most accurately describe you at your best – when you are most proud of yourself.

Day 9

List eight words that most accurately describe you at your worst – when you are least proud of yourself.

Day 10

Write about your best moral self and character. Give real-life examples of when you have been most proud of yourself by demonstrating traits such as courage, integrity, honesty, empathy, kindness, and so on.

Day 11

Write about your worst moral self and character. Give real-life examples of when you have been least proud of yourself and failed to demonstrate strong integrity, honesty, compassion, kindness, and so on.

Day 12

What are the greatest barriers to being your best moral self? For example, what factors, situations, motivators, or character traits may get in the way?

Day 13

What are your good and bad moral habits (e.g., compassionate with those who are less fortunate, thoughtful and reflective before responding or passing judgment, impatience when tired, not fully engaged with family when under stress, dismissal of others who don't support your beliefs or agenda, tempted to disregard rules or policies when they don't work in your favor)?

Days 14–15

Write your moral life story to date. Include triumphs and failures.

Days 14–15 continued

Day 16

Reflect on whether you are more of a giver or taker, more selfless or selfish. Give examples.

Day 17

Where have your categories of thinking and believing become so hardened that they may compromise your ability to listen, to be rational, to tolerate other people's opinions (about, for example, politics, ideology, religion, and so on)? Where are you most inflexible?

Day 18

Who must you forgive to unburden yourself of that unneeded weight?
Write a sample letter to that person.

Day 19

Read the previous 18 days of writing. Summarize your most important insights. *(Note this will likely take longer than 10 minutes.)*

Day 20

Five-minute gratitude writing exercise: Write all the things you are grateful for in your life.

Five-minute kindness meditation: Picture the face of someone who is exceptionally kind to you. Feel their kindness inside you.

Day 21

What is the meaning of life for you?

Day 22

What are your core beliefs about how to discern between right and wrong, and what are standards and vetting mechanisms you use to make decisions around right and wrong? Include any gray areas or times when you may flex or loosen these standards to justify your decisions or behavior or meet your personal desires.

Day 23

What are your most cherished values? Why?

Day 24

What is your Ultimate Mission – in other words, your grand reason for living?

Day 25

Seven-minute gratitude writing exercise: Write all the things you are grateful for in your life. List things you did not mention on Day 20.

Take three minutes to commit to two acts of kindness in the next seven days.

Day 26

Discuss your Performance Character assets (Performance Muscle strengths). See Appendix A for a list.

Day 27

Describe your Moral Character assets (Moral Muscle strengths). See Appendix A for a list.

Day 28

Describe your Performance Character deficiencies (Performance Muscle weaknesses).

Day 29

Describe your Moral Character deficiencies (Moral Muscle weaknesses).

Day 30

What is your true character at home and at work?

Day 31

Name two people who are leaving a brilliant legacy. Explain your choices.

Day 32

Name two people who possess the highest possible moral character. Explain your choices.

Days 33–34

Who are your real-life heroes? Explain why.

What strengths are common to your choices of the previous few days (brilliant legacy, highest moral character)?

Would you like to make someone's list? Whose?

If you have children, what would it mean to you to make their list?

Did either of your parents make your list? Why and how did they make it? What did it mean to your life?

Days 33–34 continued

Day 35

Why are you here? What value does life hold for you? What is a successful life for you?

Day 36

To what extent do your habits of eating, drinking, sleeping, and exercising compromise your ability to be your Best Moral Self?

Days 37–38

Write your tombstone epitaph. How do you want to be remembered when you are gone?

Days 37–38 continued

Days 39–40

Write your eulogy.

Days 39–40 continued

Day 41

What is the truth about your kindness at work and at home? What is the difference between being kind and being nice?

Day 42

Compassion is feeling the suffering and pain of others combined with a sincere caring for them as a person. Compassion compels action to do something about someone's suffering. (Compassion is more than kindness: It is kindness plus caring.)

What is the truth about your compassion toward others both at work and at home? How important is it to you?

Day 43

Read your writings from Days 20–42. What are your reactions? What are the important takeaways? *This exercise will take more than 10 minutes.*

Day 44

Do a compassion meditation for 10 minutes. Think of someone you know who is suffering. Put yourself in their shoes and try to feel genuine compassion for them.

Day 45

Write your Ultimate Mission again – from memory. After writing it, go back to Day 24 and compare the two.

Day 46

The epicenter of your life story is your Ultimate Mission. Refer to your writings on Days 6–7. Does the synopsis of your life story reflect your Ultimate Mission?

Days 47–48

Write about your future life story with your core beliefs, core values, and Ultimate Mission deeply embedded in the writing.

Days 47–48 continued

Day 49

What are you chasing? Why? Is the chase aligned with your deepest values and Ultimate Mission?

Day 50

Who have you become as a consequence of whatever you are chasing (e.g., achievement, fame, financial gain, love, pleasure, etc.)? A stronger, better person or one who sometimes loses touch with what matters most? A more confident, purpose-driven leader who demonstrates strong moral and ethical character or one who is just going through the motions and willing to compromise values to achieve business or personal goals? A happier, more loving spouse, partner, parent, friend – or one who is sacrificing important personal relationships?

Day 51

What were you chasing in your teenage years? How about in young adulthood? How has it changed today?

Day 52

What "scorecard" have you been using to determine your self-worth, success, and so on? To what extent has money, fame, titles, external achievements, and so on, factored into your assessments?

Day 53

Are your energy investments on a daily, weekly, monthly basis aligned with your core values and Ultimate Mission?

Days 54–56

For the next three days, turn your awareness inward to the tone and content of your Private Voice. On Day 54, give your general observations about how you speak to yourself. Is the voice warm, critical, wise, helpful, supportive, brutal, jaded, and so on? Would you be proud to make its message and tone public? Whose voice from your past does it most reflect? Would you want to speak to people you care about the way your Private Voice speaks to you?

Day 55

Write from memory how your Inner Voice spoke to you throughout the previous day (Day 54) . . .

Day 56

Do the same thing as you did for Day 55.

Reflect on the tone and message of the way you coach yourself.

Day 57

Would you want those you care most about to have your Inner Voice inside their heads? What would you want the tone and message of their Inner Voice to be?

Day 58

How important is your Private Voice to your quest to live the highest moral life possible? To what extent should character strengths be applied to your inner coaching voice?

Day 59

To what extent are your Public and Private Voices fully aligned in tone and message? Write about your authenticity. Are your Public and Private Voices very different?

Day 60

To what extent does your Private Voice reflect your core values and Ultimate Mission in life? How important is this issue? How important are the tone and content of your Private Voice to your ability to lead with character?[2]

---

[2] The best way to retrain your Private Voice, from our decades of work at the Institute, is to intentionally script it through daily writing. Intentionally script how you want your Private Voice to speak to you when various situations arise. Grade yourself daily on the performance of your new Inner Voice. As mentioned earlier in the book, your Private Voice should speak to you, council you, coach you in the same way you would advise someone you deeply care about. The voice can be compassionate, kind, challenging, tough-minded, stern, forceful, etc., depending on the situation. Once your Personal Credo is built and downloaded into your cognitive and emotional operating system, it becomes your reference guide for all your self-coaching. Your Personal Credo is your ultimate resource for wisdom.

Day 61

Review your writings from Days 43–60 and summarize the most important takeaways.

Day 62

For two minutes, meditate on your breathing in and breathing out. If your mind wanders, very gently bring it back to your breathing.

For eight minutes, write one thank-you letter and send it in the next three days.

Day 63

What is the truth about the strength of your integrity muscle? To what extent do you act on what you determine is the right thing for you? Give examples from the last several days of how you have exercised your muscle of integrity.

Day 64

Who are the people who have hurt you the most? Do you still hold a grudge? What advantages does holding a grudge bring to you? How does your Best Moral Self advise you?

Day 65

What is the truth about the strength of your patience muscle? Who do you show the most impatience with? Are they people you care about the most? What does it feel like when people you care about are impatient with you? When people are impatient with you, does it help or hurt your confidence?

Day 66

Go to Appendix B and complete the forced ranking of 12 moral character traits. What are your self-acknowledged top strengths and weaknesses?

Days 67–68

Develop a plan for growing your two weakest character muscles (which were identified in yesterday's forced-ranking questionnaire).

Days 67–68 continued

Days 69–70

How honest and trustworthy are you? Do you always tell the truth? Keep track of how many partial or full falsehoods you have spoken in the last two days. Explain your reasons. Do you believe it's okay to tell "white lies"?

Days 69–70 continued

Day 71

Empathy is the capacity to put yourself in the shoes of others and feel and think the way they do. Their thoughts and feelings are triggered inside you. What is the strength of your empathy muscle?

Day 72

Full engagement is the acquired ability to give your full and best energy to whatever you are doing, right here, right now. The opposite is multi-tasking. How often are you fully engaged at work and at home? Who gets your full engagement – and who doesn't? In keeping with your core values, who should be the recipient of this supreme gift?

Day 73

Review your writings from Days 62–72 and write down the most significant insights.

Day 74

How generous are you? What's the size of your generosity muscle? How important is this for you? Give examples of how you exercise your generosity muscle on a regular basis.

Day 75

Are you a courageous person? Do you act in accordance with your beliefs despite the risks or negative consequences? How would you show courage at work and at home?

Day 76

Are you tough-minded? Can you resist being adversely influenced by the power of the thinking and emotional pushing of others? Will you change your thinking to please others or to gain a professional advantage?

Days 77–78

Are you fair and just? How do you show fairness at work and at home? Do others perceive you to be fair-minded, or do you play politics over fairness? Do you treat some of your direct reports more favorably than others? How about family members? Are you manipulative? Give examples from work and home.

Days 77–78 continued

Day 79

What is the strength of your positivity muscle? Are you largely an optimist or pessimist? Does it matter at work or at home? What would others likely say about your positivity strength? How does your Private Voice factor into your positive or negative emotional bearing?

Day 80

Are you a resilient person? How quickly can you rebound from set-backs? How often can you intentionally turn disappointments into opportunities for learning and growth?

Day 81

What is your capacity for critical, logical thinking? Can you set aside emotions when appropriate and successfully initiate a logical train of thought? Is your critical thinking ability too often overwhelmed by strong emotion? Give examples of your ability to think clearly in a stressful environment.

Days 82–89

1. Construct your Personal Credo. From the building blocks set forth in Days 1–81, create the most precise articulation of mission success of your life that you are capable of providing right now. There are no right or wrong answers. You are defining how you intend to live your life and your rules of engagement, regardless of what happens. This document will likely require many rewrites. Read what you have written on the previous days and keep writing until you're willing to bet your life on it. Things to consider in creating your Personal Credo:

   a. Ultimate Mission

   b. Best Self and Best Moral Self

   c. Hierarchy of values

   d. People you love and cherish most

   e. Hierarchy of beliefs

   f. Meaning of life

   g. How you want to be remembered as a person

   h. Leadership legacy

   i. Eulogy

   j. Commitments you intend to act on with your precious gift of life

   k. How you intend to keep score going forward

   l. Share and discuss your Personal Credo with someone you love.

   m. Construct a scorecard to measure how you are doing. It can be as simple or complex as you want it to be. Just make sure to record what you do or fail to do on a daily basis. The loading of this document into your moral operating system and building habits to support it will occur in Days 91–150. You will use the same 10-minute daily journal writing to accomplish both of these.[3]

---

[3] You may wonder why examples of Personal Credos from our clients have not been provided here. Experience has shown us that examples have too much influence over our thinking. Rather than creating something completely original and authentic, we pick and choose what we like from the work of others. A Personal Credo must be uniquely crafted in a way that you alone could author. It can be 1 paragraph or 10, specific or general. This sacred document must be totally your creation.

Days 82–89 continued

Days 82–89 continued

Days 82–89 continued

Days 82–89 continued

Days 82–89 continued

Days 82–89 continued

Days 82–89 continued

Days 82–89 continued

Day 90

Commit to using your Personal Credo to navigate through the countless moral challenges you will face in the future. Your pledge to do so is acknowledged with your signature.

_____   _____

Signature   Date

Embedding Your Personal Credo and Supporting It with Habits
(Days 91–150)

Most of life is controlled by habit, and clearly human beings are creatures of habit. The next 59 days of writing and energy investment are designed to further strengthen the critical habits that will enable you to be your best moral self and the person you most desire to be. The more energy investments and the more precise the investments in things like kindness, humility, integrity, and so on, the more available they will be to you. Robust strengths of character – both performance and moral – form the bedrock of your Personal Credo. The intentional investment of your time and energy over the next four weeks will provide an unparalleled return in your efforts to lead with character in all dimensions of your life, and to achieve your desired life and leadership legacy.

Day 91

1. Has journal writing for 10 minutes a day become a habit for you?

2. How do you know?

Using the same formula, map out a new habit you would like to build in support of your Personal Credo.

Day 92

Select a trigger word or image that will call forth your Personal Credo whenever you are confronted with an ethical situation.

For me, it's the voice of my mother saying, "Do the right thing." My mother was the personification of goodness to me. I've conditioned her words to immediately summon my Personal Credo.

– Dr. Jim Loehr

Rehearse using your trigger word or image in each of the following situations: You're tempted to (1) cheat on something; (2) tell a lie; (3) be rude or dismissive to someone.

Day 93

Memorize the following moral deliberation process called FHGD:

Step 1: What are the facts (F)?

Step 2: What does your heart (H) say?

Step 3: What does your gut (G) say?

Step 4: Make your decision (D) based on these data points.

Apply these four steps to an ethical situation you're now facing. Write your answers in your journal to all four steps.

Day 94

Practice projecting the worst possible consequence of a moral action compared to the best possible consequence. This reflection can provide critical input into your moral deliberation. Project the worst and best consequences for each of the following scenarios:

1. Consistently speeding 20+ mph over the posted limit

2. Having an affair

3. Strategically inflating your expense report

4. Exaggerating the truth in your storytelling to garner support for your project

Day 95

Write your Personal Credo from memory. What is your trigger word or image that best calls your Credo forward?

Day 96

For five minutes, do a kindness meditation. While breathing slowly and deeply, imagine displaying kindness to everyone you meet.

For five minutes, do a gratitude exercise by writing all the small things in life you are grateful for.

Day 97

Integrity is doing what you judge to be the right and honorable thing. It represents 50% of our morality. Give three examples from this past week of how you acted with integrity – or decidedly did *not* act that way.

Day 98

Your spouse/life partner asks you if you went out for a beer with colleagues after a long day at a conference. Your spouse/partner is terribly jealous. If you tell him/her the truth, it will likely result in a big crisis and lots of wasted time and energy. Use the four steps in FHGD to decide. Write out your answer to all the steps. According to your Credo, what should you do?

Day 99

You witnessed a colleague clearly violating an important company safety policy. This person is a close friend. Should you report the incident? There will likely be serious consequences for the violation. Would you act differently if you had a strong dislike for the person? Consider the following:

1. Use your trigger word or image and summon your Personal Credo.

2. Answer the four questions in FHGD (Facts, Heart, Gut, Decide).

3. Project best and worst consequences. Put your thoughts and decision in writing.

Day 100

Read everything you have written for Days 91–99. Write about your thoughts and feelings from the reading.

Day 101

Reflect on whether you are more of a "giver" or "taker" in life. Complete the questionnaire in Appendix C. Count the number of boxes checked on the giver side and compare that with those checked on the taker side. Leading with character requires that you check off more than 13 or more boxes on the giver side. Does your total box count align with how you see yourself? With your gut response? With your "crap detector"? Return to the boxes checked on the taker side and do some soulful reflection.

Day 102

Review your responses to the Giver versus Taker questionnaire and write about any improvements you would consider making.

Day 103

Justice Louis D. Brandeis once made the statement, "Sunlight is said to be the best of disinfectants." Where in your character do you need more sunlight to shine through? In other words, where in your character do you need a good dose of "face-the-truth"? Let sunlight in by writing about it.

Day 104

Give an example from your life where your moral "crap detector" failed you. Give an example of when it worked perfectly. Do you sense this asset is sharpening and strengthening from your journal writing?

Day 105

Reflect on the extent to which the message and tone of your Private Voice is aligned with your Best Moral Self and Personal Credo. To what extent is your character revealed in the silent language of your Inner Voice?

Day 106

Give examples of how your Private Voice both supports and compromises your efforts to be your Best Moral Self and to lead with character.

Day 107

Make a list of positive habits you would like to acquire that would enable you to more fully live your Personal Credo. Examples might include saying "stop" to yourself every time you start to say or do something not aligned with your credo; saying "fully present" when with your children to stimulate higher levels of engagement; or saying "no spinning" to prompt you to more fully align your storytelling with the truth.

Day 108

Choose one habit from the list you made on Day 107 and initiate the habit acquisition process. Apply H = PTR³*. Write your plan out in detail. (Remember: Full habit formation typically takes from 20 to 60 days.)

---

*H=Habit, P=Purpose, T=Trigger Word, R3=Response, Reward, Repeat.

Day 109

Apply what you have learned to the following moral dilemma: You believe the tactics your business team is planning to employ to gain market share crosses ethical lines. Raising an ethical concern could have real consequences in your being promoted; you might even get terminated. How should you respond? Write about the process you will use to make your decision.

Day 110

An important step to prevent our moral judgment from being hijacked is to recognize when we block or disregard information contrary to the outcome we really want ("motivated reasoning"). It happens constantly in politics. Facts are distorted, bent, altered, or ignored to support a political position.

Give two examples in your past of how you justified a moral decision using motivated reasoning.

Day 111

Meditate for five minutes. For the first two, focus on your breathing in and out. When your mind wanders, bring your attention back gently to your breathing. For the next three minutes, continue your meditation but focus on compassion. Picture the face of someone who has shown great compassion for you. Attempt to feel compassion for those you know are suffering.

Spend five minutes writing about your capacity for compassion and the extent to which you would like your capacity expanded.

Day 112

Consider this: You are married with three young children. You are asked to make an overnight trip with a colleague who is also married with children. At dinner, unexpectedly, romantic sparks fly in both directions. You invite her to your room to pick up some papers and she responds that she would be happy to get the papers but is hopeful there will be much more. She then says, "No one will ever know." You are tempted. You have only seconds to respond. Provide your moral decision-making process in writing. To what extent do trigger words and images, risk/reward consequences, and Personal Credo values help in your instant decision?

Day 113

Confidence and humility must be properly balanced. Too much confidence without humility breeds arrogance; too much humility without confidence breeds insecurity. What is the truth about the balance of these two character muscles for you? From what you've learned, how would you build strength in confidence? How would you build strength in humility?

Day 114

A direct report has been struggling with family problems for six months. His work performance has seriously suffered. You've had several conversations with him about this. One of his children has a serious illness, and he lost both of his parents in a car crash. Should you find a replacement for him? Your boss is putting pressure on you to do something. Use the four-step FHGD process to make your decision. Is it fully aligned with your Personal Credo?

Day 115

Consider your worst moral failures. In retrospect, what was the flawed process that allowed these to occur? What changes must occur in you so that they never happen again?

Day 116

You find yourself tempted to omit a critical piece of information from your report because it could be a big embarrassment to your boss. The report is due tomorrow.

1. Ignite your Personal Credo with your trigger word or image.
2. Do the risk/reward analysis.
3. Make your decision.

Day 117

Imagine one or two moral dilemmas you are likely to face soon. Apply to each what you have learned and write about how you should resolve each.

Day 118

A jealous colleague makes a snide comment about your political beliefs in a staff meeting in front of the entire division. You are embarrassed and angry. How should your Best Moral Self handle this?

Day 119

The character strength that balances love/empathy is tough-mindedness. Reflect first on your capacity for loving others. Next reflect on your capacity to feel empathy – to feel and think the way others do. Last, reflect on when and how you display tough-mindedness. Which of the three muscles needs to be strengthened most? From what you have learned, how would you strengthen that character muscle?

Day 120

Read everything you have written for Days 101–119. Summarize your thoughts and feelings.

Day 121

If you have strong religious beliefs, does your Personal Credo reflect them? Write about your religious thoughts, feelings, and values. How accepting are you of the religious beliefs of others, particularly when those beliefs are not aligned with yours?

Day 122

You've been asked to downsize your department by 20% to make year-end numbers. You strongly believe it is an unethical thing to do. If you balk at all, you will likely be replaced as part of the downsizing because some already perceive you as soft. Should you make your case and risk losing your job? You are to announce the shakeup to your department in five days. Write about your decision-making process. Include the following things:

1. Activate the trigger word or image that calls forth your Personal Credo.

2. Analyze from your credo perspective.

3. Analyze using FHGD.

4. Analyze using risk/reward consequences.

5. Make your decision.

Day 123

For five minutes, do a loving/kindness meditation. Picture the face of the person who has been the most loving, most kind person to you in your life. Feel the love and kindness inside you. For five minutes, write about the experience.

Day 124

Your boss makes you feel inadequate and incompetent. You have always had trouble with strong, aggressive authority figures. You strongly resent your boss for all the misery and discomfort he puts you through. You love the firm you work for and don't want to quit. What's the morally right thing for you to do? What does your credo say?

Day 125

Write about any positive changes that have occurred in your life as a result of your daily journal writing for the last 124 days. Has your treatment of others improved in any way? Are you beginning to feel better prepared to handle moral dilemmas?

Day 126

What do you need more of in your life to bring you to a higher level of happiness and fulfillment? Connect your answer to your Ultimate Mission in life.

Day 127

Your boss believes you were the person responsible for making the big deal happen. In reality, it was another member of your team who landed the client and got the ball rolling in the first place. Should you let your boss know? You have a meeting with her in an hour. Write out your deliberation process and make your decision.

Day 128

Give examples of how you are using your power to help others. To what extent is your moral identity that of a loving, caring, compassionate person?

Day 129

On Day 108, you chose a habit to actively build, using the formula $H = PTR^3$. How are you doing? Have you been making the necessary investments of your energy? If things are progressing positively, select another habit to acquire that will be supportive to your Personal Credo. Refer to the list you made on Day 107.

Day 130

Select a new habit from Day 107 that you wish to acquire and apply PTR^3 to, in as much detail as possible. Launch the process as soon as you are ready.

Day 131

Read everything you have written for Days 121–130. Summarize your thoughts and feelings from the reading.

Day 132

Your team is under intense pressure to expand the benefits of a new drug the company is about to launch. Your boss directs you to be "more creative" in your benefits language. The clinical evidence is not there. Use all the tools you have been working on to decide how to respond. Write about your deliberation process.

Day 133

A particular person in your firm drives you crazy. You're not sure why; he just does. You go out of your way to make life difficult for him, to make fun of him. Since initiating your daily writing, you're starting to feel guilty. What should you do based on your credo, the FHGD formula, and risk/reward projections? Detail your thinking in writing.

Day 134

Reflect on any ethical situation you encountered in the last two days. What was it how did you respond? Were you satisfied with your judgment and your response?

Day 135

You've joined a firm where corporate misconduct is commonplace, and you are expected to join in. You've been out of work for more than a year before landing this job. Your family is just beginning to get back on its feet financially. Quitting the job would be devastating, but the culture is clearly immoral. What is the right thing for you to do? Detail your judgment process.

Day 136

You've invested approximately 22½ hours thus far, spread over 135 days, to strengthen your moral character. Write about key insights, learnings, and personal growth realized from the investment.

Day 137

You've acquired confidential information that would give your firm a tremendous competitive advantage. You would likely become a hero if you let your CEO know. You pledged the person you heard it from to keep the matter confidential, but there is absolutely no way any leak can be traced back to you. You have three days to decide. Use all the tools provided to make your decision and act on it. Write down your entire deliberation process.

Day 138

Under what circumstances does your Best Moral Self become compromised? When are you likely to fail in your treatment of others? What can you do about it?

Day 139

Your boss has communicated confidentially that the firm is being sold and the division you lead will likely be eliminated. You will be fine – the new owners will likely move you to another part of the business. All your direct reports will lose their jobs if the sale goes through. The deal is 95% done. You immediately want to let your staff know what's about to happen so that they can prepare themselves. You deeply care about them. You were told not to tell anyone. What should you do to protect your people? What does a person with integrity do? Write out your analysis in detail.

Day 140

Do you believe evil exists in the world? Why are good people vulnerable to corruption, and willing to bring so much pain and suffering into the lives of others? How has your thinking about this evolved since you started journal writing?

Day 141

You're one of three top executives empowered to look at emission control data and come up with a real-world solution that allows the company to meet its financial goals. The implicit assignment is to find ways to manipulate the data to avoid prosecution or fines. How should you respond? Detail your deliberation process in writing and make your decision.

Day 142

Read everything you have written since Day 132 and summarize your thoughts and feelings from the reading.

Day 143

On a 360-degree report, several people provided feedback that you consistently show favoritism to certain people. What should you do about it, if anything? Does this qualify as an ethical issue? Explain your answer.

Day 144

You've been asked to serve on a Fortune 50 board, but it will mean an additional six to eight days away from family each year, and your current position already requires you to travel an enormous amount. Serving on the board is something you've always wanted. What should you do? Consult your Personal Credo and Ultimate Mission as primary inputs into your decision-making process. What does your heart say? What does your gut say?

Day 145

You are to make a report to your sales division in 30 minutes. A colleague has publicly embarrassed you several times when he/she had the stage. That colleague has lost two important clients in the last month. This is your chance to even the score. You are tempted. What should you do? Use all your tools to get to the right decision. Detail your deliberation process in writing.

Day 146

A major objective of this training program is to raise your awareness of whenever and wherever you enter moral territory. As that happens, you are cued to mobilize all the tools you have acquired to respond properly. This is called "context cueing." Tools include (1) calling forth specific words, images, and phrases; (2) summoning your Personal Credo; (3) looking at the facts (F), your heart (H), your gut (G); and (4) considering risk/reward issues. Write about whether this has been happening with you. Give specific examples.

Day 147

Repeated intentional energy investments represent the best strategy for building and maintaining a strong moral brain. We get back what we invest our energy in, for better or worse. What investments, intentional or not, have you made in the past that have compromised your moral character? Where should you make investments going forward to get the moral brain you want?

Day 148

Give two practical examples of how your daily training has improved your ability to lead with character.

Day 149

List the most important insights you have gained from the 150-day training program so far. Visualize each of the insights being implemented in your life.

Day 150

Congratulations! You have completed 25 hours over five months of training to strengthen your ability to lead with character. The hope is that you will continue some form of this training on a regular basis for the rest of your life.

The stakes are too high for you and everyone around you. Write any new and important commitments you are willing to make going forward. When finished, sign your name below and date it.

_____   _____

Signature   Date

ADDITIONAL PAGE FOR JOURNAL WRITING

ADDITIONAL PAGE FOR JOURNAL WRITING

....

....

....

....

....

....

....

....

....

....

....

....

....

....

....

....

....

....

....

....

....

....

....

....

....

ADDITIONAL PAGE FOR JOURNAL WRITING

ADDITIONAL PAGE FOR JOURNAL WRITING

....

....

....

....

....

....

....

....

....

....

....

....

....

....

....

....

....

....

....

....

....

....

....

....

....

....

ADDITIONAL PAGE FOR JOURNAL WRITING

Additional Page for Journal Writing

ADDITIONAL PAGE FOR JOURNAL WRITING

ADDITIONAL PAGE FOR JOURNAL WRITING

ADDITIONAL PAGE FOR JOURNAL WRITING

ADDITIONAL PAGE FOR JOURNAL WRITING

ADDITIONAL PAGE FOR JOURNAL WRITING

ADDITIONAL PAGE FOR JOURNAL WRITING

ADDITIONAL PAGE FOR JOURNAL WRITING

ADDITIONAL PAGE FOR JOURNAL WRITING

ADDITIONAL PAGE FOR JOURNAL WRITING

ADDITIONAL PAGE FOR JOURNAL WRITING

ADDITIONAL PAGE FOR JOURNAL WRITING

ADDITIONAL PAGE FOR JOURNAL WRITING

ADDITIONAL PAGE FOR JOURNAL WRITING

Appendix A: Character Traits

Every one of these character strengths – either performance strengths (P) or moral strengths (M) – is an acquired disposition.

1. Adaptability: You adjust well to changing conditions (performance strength (P)).

2. Adventurous Spirit: You seek exciting challenges for personal exploration (P).

3. Affection: You openly show warmth and caring toward others (moral strength (M)).

4. Ambition: You are goal-oriented and goal-directed (P).

5. Authenticity: Your Public and Private Voices are aligned; you are genuine (M).

6. Compassion: You feel a deep, abiding concern for the suffering of others, combined with the aspiration to do something to relieve it (M).

7. Competitiveness: You enjoy pitting your skills against the skills of others (P).

8. Confidence: You believe in your abilities (P).

9. Creativity: You generate original, spontaneous thinking and solutions (P).

10. Critical Thinking: You think in a reality-based way (P).

11. Curiosity: You are inquisitive; you want to understand how things work (P).

12. Decisiveness: You make definitive choices (P).

13. Dependability: You can be counted on to meet your commitments (M).

14. Determination/Persistence/Grit: You rally your strength of will to overcome obstacles; you refuse to give up (P).

15. Discernment: You seek the deeper causes of things (P).

16. Empathy: You experience what others are thinking and feeling (M).

17. Engagement with Others: You bring your full and best energy to the present moment in your interactions with others (M).

18. Focus: You can control your attention (P).

19. Forgiveness: You are able to clear the record for those who have harmed you (M).

20. Fortitude: You fight relentlessly for what's right (P).

21. Generosity: You share whatever you have with others (M).

22. Gratitude: You feel sincere appreciation for what you have (M).

23. Honor: Your actions and decisions reflect the highest ethical standards (M).

24. Humility: You are modest and highly aware of your shortcomings (M).

25. Humor: You can laugh at yourself and the ironies of life (P).

26. Justice: You are fair in your dealings with others (M).

27. Kindness/Love/Care: You have a deep regard and affection for others (M).

28. Love of Learning: You find joy in discovering new things (P).

29. Loyalty: You are faithful to your friends, family, and associates (M).

30. Moral Courage: You act in accordance with what you believe is right despite any risk or negative consequences to you or to others (M).

31. Moral Integrity: You act in accordance with what you judge to be right (M).

32. Motivation: You energize yourself to act (P).

33. Open-Mindedness: You are receptive to new ideas and thoughts (P).

34. Optimism: You generate strong belief and faith in a positive future (P).

35. Organization: You are orderly (P).

36. Patience: You accept imperfections in others (M).

37. Personal Courage: You act in accordance with what you believe is the right thing to do despite any risks or negative consequences to you (P).

38. Positivity: You view the world through the eyes of opportunity rather than survival (P).

39. Prudence: You exercise good judgment (P).

40. Punctuality: You honor time commitments (P).

41. Resiliency: You bounce back from disappointment or loss (P).

42. Respect: You treat everyone with dignity (M).

43. Seeking Challenges: You constantly look for ways to expand current limits by stepping outside your comfort zone (P).

44. Self-Awareness: You have reality-based perceptions of yourself (P).

45. Self-Control/Willpower: You mobilize the necessary energy to exercise restraint over your impulses, desires, and emotions, and to fulfill your intentions (P).

46. Tough-Mindedness/Mental Toughness: You control your thoughts; you are mentally strong and focused (P).

47. Trust: You believe in the basic goodness of others (M).

48. Truthfulness: You accurately report events and facts as you know them (M).

49. Vitality/Vigor: You feel energetic; you feel enthusiasm for life (P).

50. Wisdom: You formulate insights into the deeper meaning of life (P).

Appendix B: Ranking Your Character Traits

How well do these 12 character traits/muscles "hold up" when you experience high stress – anger, fear, fatigue, pressure, low confidence, and so on? Order them as they relate to you, from weakest (1 – most likely to fail under stress) to strongest (12 – least likely).

_____ Loving, kind, and caring (having a deep regard and affection for others)

_____ Respect (treating everyone with dignity)

_____ Patience (being tolerant of the imperfections of others)

_____ Generosity (sharing whatever you have with others)

_____ Gratitude (feeling sincere appreciation for what you have)

_____ Humility (being modest and highly aware of your shortcomings)

_____ Compassion (feeling a deep, abiding concern for the suffering of others, combined with the aspiration to do something to relieve it)

_____ Truthfulness, honesty (reporting events and facts as accurately as you know them)

_____ Trust (believing in the basic goodness of others)

_____ Engagement (bringing your best energy to the present moment in your interactions with others)

_____ Moral integrity (acting in accordance with what you judge to be "right")

_____ Authenticity (aligning your Public and Private Voice; genuineness)

Appendix C: Giver versus Taker Scale*

1. Other-focused   Self-focused

2. Driven to help others succeed   Driven to achieve personal success

3. Compassion, kindness, empathy-directed   Winning, power, money-directed

4. Concerned about the impact you have on others   Concerned about making a good impression on others

5. Love to help others become better   Love to find ways to help yourself become better

6. Give energy to others   Take energy from others

7. Exude gratitude for all you have   Never seem to be satisfied with what you have

---

*The Giver versus Taker scale was constructed by the author from the writings of Adam Grant and others.

8. Love to mentor others   Love to be mentored by others

9. Welfare of others comes first   Your welfare comes first

10. Give credit when successful   Take credit when successful

11. Motivate others   Motivate self

12. Protect others   Protect self

13. Focus on who the employee is as a   Focus on the employee's
    person first   contribution to the
                                                        business first

14. Give the spotlight away   Love to be in the spotlight

15. Praise others   Seek praise from others

16. Comfortable expressing vul-   Uncomfortable expressing
    nerability   vulnerability

17. Encourage and invite input from   Encourage and invite only positive
    others – pro and con   input from others

18. Seek collaboration   Seek independence

19. More people-centered   More process-centered

20. Take the blame   Blame others